Text by Elena Pasquali
Illustrations copyright © 2008, 2009, 2011, 2012 Nicola Smee
This edition copyright © 2014 Lion Hudson

Published by Lion Children's Books
an imprint of
Lion Hudson plc
Wilkinson House, Jordan Hill Road,
Oxford OX2 8DR, England
www.lionhudson.com/lionchildrens
ISBN 978 0 7459 6489 8

Stories originally published in *Two-Minute Bible Stories*, *The Lion Book of
Two-Minute Parables*, and *The Lion Book of Two-Minute Christmas Stories*.

First edition 2014

A catalogue record for this book is available from the British Library

Printed and bound in China, June 2014, LH17

The Lion Little Book of
Bible Stories

Retold by Elena Pasquali *Illustrated by* Nicola Smee

LION
CHILDREN'S

All things bright and beautiful,
All creatures great and small,
All things wise and wonderful,
The Lord God made them all.

Cecil Frances Alexander (1818–95)

Contents

In the Beginning

In the dark and shapeless nothing, God spoke.

Light

And there was the first bright, sparkling daytime.

On the second day, God spoke again.

Sky

And there was a dome of blue above a glittering sea.

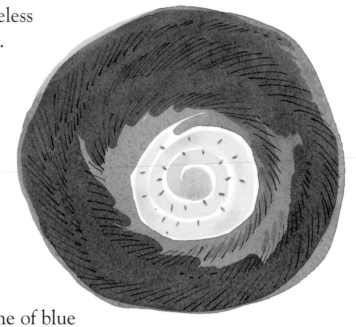

On the third day, God's voice was
quiet and low.

Earth

And there was good brown earth,
tiny seedlings, waving corn, and
tall, tall trees.

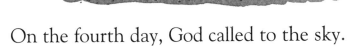

On the fourth day, God called to the sky.

Shine

In the daytime, the sun shone bright
and gold.

In the night-time, the moon shone silver.
Tiny stars twinkled all around.

twinkle

On the fifth day, God sang:

Come alive

Fish swam in the seas and birds flew through the air.

On the sixth day, God's voice rang out again. Animals came rustling through the forests and running over the plains and leaping across the mountains.

In a kindly voice, God said:

Friend

The boy and the girl smiled.
"You are special to me," said God. "Your children will be special to me… and your grandchildren, and your great grandchildren, and their children's children for ever."

On the seventh day, God only whispered as the sun came up.

Rest

It was a day to enjoy the wonderful world.

Noah and the Flood

L ong ago, on a sunny day, God came to talk to Noah.
"I'm sad about the world," said God. "It has all gone wrong."
"I know," said Noah. "It's people. They can be so bad."
"And so," said God, "I'm going to send a flood. It will end the old world. Then I will start again."
"Oh dear," said Noah. "Whatever will I do?"
"You will build a boat," replied God.
"Will I?" asked Noah.
"You will take your family on board," said God.

"And you will take the animals on board, two of every kind."

"How will I do that?" asked Noah. He sounded worried.

"I'll help," said God cheerfully. "Then I will send the rain."

And God did.

It rained and rained and rained.

The flood came up. The boat floated away.

"Is it ever going to stop raining?" asked Noah.

God did not say anything.

pitter patter
splish splish

Inside the boat, Noah tried to be cheerful.

"God hasn't forgotten us," he announced.

But he was beginning to wonder.

Then one day...

"We're aground," cried Noah.

bump!

14

coo

He spoke to the dove: "Go and look for land.
We can't stay here for ever."
The dove flew away and the dove came back.
In its beak was a fresh green twig.
"That's good news," said Noah. "It means the flood is going down."

When the land was dry, at last God spoke.
"Leave the boat," said God. "Make the whole world new.
"The rainbow is my promise.
Never again will I flood the world.
I will keep it safe for ever."

roar

Moses and the Deep Water

The great river of Egypt was deep. Among the rushes was a floating basket.

quack

A baby boy

A princess of Egypt came to bathe. She looked inside the floating basket.

"Poor little Hebrew baby. The king of Egypt wants to harm the Hebrew babies. A mother is trying to save her son.

"Well, I shall keep him safe now. And I shall give him a name: Moses.

"But I need someone to take care of him!"
A little girl stepped out from the rushes.
The princess guessed who: baby Moses' sister.
"I know someone," said the girl.
The princess was delighted.

My little one

The little girl brought her mother. She
was, of course, the baby's mother too.
So Moses was safe from the water.

When Moses grew up, he found out about the wicked king. He found out that the Hebrew people were the king's slaves. He found out that they were treated very badly.

Oof!

When he tried to help, he got into trouble. He had to run away from Egypt.

Moses

In the wild country, he saw a strange thing: a bush was on fire, but it wasn't burning up. As he looked, he heard a voice.

It was God. God told Moses to go to the king of Egypt. "Tell him to let the Hebrew people go free," said God.

Moses went and asked.
The king was angry.

No, no, no

But God wanted the Hebrews to go free.
Nothing went right for the king or for Egypt
till at last he changed his mind.

Moses led his people out of Egypt.
They reached a sea. God spoke to Moses:
   "Lift up your stick."
   When Moses lifted his stick, the waters moved aside.
They left a path through the sea.
   Moses and the Hebrews were safe from the water.
   God had set them free.

On we go!

19

Jonah and the Whale

J onah was a prophet. If God told him something,
it was his job to pass the message on. Right now,
God was telling Jonah to warn the people of Nineveh.
"Tell them to stop being bad, or I will have to
punish them."

Goodbye!

Jonah did not want to obey.
He wanted to see the people
of Nineveh punished.
He ran down to the sea.
He got on a boat bound
for far, far away.

In the night, God sent a storm. The sailors were very afraid.

"It's all my fault," wailed Jonah. "I've disobeyed God. Throw me into the sea, and the storm will stop."

Man overboard!

God still wanted Jonah to go to Nineveh. God sent a whale, who swallowed Jonah.

GULP

The whale spat Jonah out onto a beach.

splodge

Jonah hurried to Nineveh.
He called aloud to everyone to change their ways.
The people of Nineveh listened to all he said. "We have been bad," they wept. "We must change our ways."
The king of Nineveh was saddest of all. He gave an order.

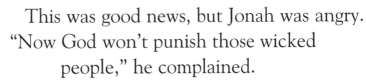

This was good news, but Jonah was angry. "Now God won't punish those wicked people," he complained.

Hmmph

As he sulked, a plant grew up. It gave lovely shade.

In the night a worm came and ate it. Jonah was sadder than ever.

Hooray

baa

"So you care for a plant, do you? Well, I care for the people of Nineveh. And their children. And their animals."

23

Daniel and the Lions

King Darius was in charge of a huge empire.
He needed wise people to help him.

The wisest of all was Daniel. So King Darius
gave him the most important job.

That made other people angry.

"We must get rid of him," said one.

"I've an idea," said another.

Well done

*whisper
whisper*

They went to the king.

"O King, may you live for ever," they began. "May everyone obey you and worship you and you alone, O great and most wonderful king."

The king was pleased.

"You must make a new law. Say that anyone who worships anyone but you will be punished. Say they will be thrown to the lions."

The king made the law.

The men hurried off to find Daniel.

"There he is," they said. "He's saying prayers to his God. That's against the law."

Dear God...

King Darius was most upset. He was sad to see Daniel thrown to the lions. "The law wasn't about you," he sobbed.

God did not want Daniel hurt. God sent an angel to stop the lions from eating him.

King Darius worried about Daniel all through the night. Then he went back to the den of lions.

Shhh
Go to sleep

roar

He called out to Daniel. "Are you alright?"

Daniel answered. "God has heard all my prayers," he said. "God has taken care of me."

I'm fine

ZZZ

27

Jesus is Born

L ong ago, in Nazareth, lived a woman named Mary. She was sitting dreaming of the day she would marry Joseph. Suddenly, an angel appeared.

"God has chosen you to be the mother of his Son," said the angel. "You will name him 'Jesus'."

"I will," said Mary.

An angel also spoke
to Joseph, and he
agreed to take care of
Mary and her baby.

Together they went to Bethlehem.
"I'm sorry we have to go on a long
journey when the baby is soon to be
born," he said, "but the emperor
has ordered everyone to their
hometown for his people-count."

clip clop

They reached Bethlehem late in the day. To their dismay, there was no room in the inn.

"But we can make ourselves comfortable in this stable," Joseph explained to Mary.

There, where the donkey shuffled and the ox munched, Mary's baby Jesus was born.

shhhh

There were some shepherds out on the hills that night, watching over their sheep.

Suddenly an angel appeared.

"Don't be afraid," said the angel. "I have good news. God's Son has been born in Bethlehem. One day, he will rescue people from all their troubles; tonight, he is cradled in a manger in Bethlehem."

Around the messenger a host of angels sang.

Peace on earth

Then the sky went dark.

"Well," said the shepherds, "we must make our sheep safe and go!"

They hurried to Bethlehem and found the stable by the lamp that flickered within.

They found the baby wrapped in swaddling clothes and lying in a manger.

The Wise Men

Look!

The men who studied the stars lived in a country far to the east.

"See that star – shining so brightly?" said one.

"I have never seen it before," said the second.

"It must surely be a sign from heaven," said the third.

They went and studied their books of lore and learning.

"The Jewish people are waiting for God to send them a great king," they all agreed.

"The star is the sign of his birth."

"We must go and find him."

They set out with rich gifts, journeying always at night so the star could be their guide. It led them over the lonely miles to the great city of the Jews: Jerusalem. Inside its walls they began asking questions. "Do you know where we can find the newborn king?"

The townsfolk were puzzled.

In his palace, King Herod was angry. "The emperor himself made me king of the Jews," he muttered.

"I will not allow a rival."

He went to consult his advisers. Then he ordered his servants to bring the men to a secret meeting. He scowled as they told him of their quest. But he had a plan.

"I can help," he said. "The holy books of the Jewish people tell of a king who is to come. God's chosen king will be born in Bethlehem.

"Go there," he whispered, "and then come and tell me where he is. I shall have to go and show him the respect he deserves."

The men set off. As before, the star lit the way. It led them to Bethlehem.

There they found Jesus.

"We bring our tribute to the king," they said, as they unwrapped their gifts: gold, frankincense, and myrrh.

frankincense

myrrh

gold

An angel told the men not to return to Herod, for he meant to harm the child. In a dream, an angel also told Joseph to flee with his family: for Jesus was God's chosen king, and he would grow up to bring people into God's kingdom.

Jairus and His Daughter

Jairus was wiping his tears as he hurried along the street. "She's very ill and getting worse," he said. "My darling daughter."

Jairus hurried to meet Jesus.

"I've heard you can make sick people well," he said. "Please come and make my daughter well."

It's horrid being ill

I hope she gets better

Jesus agreed to come.

But they could hardly move for the crowds.

And Jesus even stopped to help someone else.

Please help me

Oh dear

Poor
girl

At last Jesus and Jairus reached the house.

Women were weeping and wailing.

"What's the fuss about?" asked Jesus. "She's not dead."

He went to the room where the little girl lay.

She was pale and cold.

He took her hand and spoke to her.

Little girl,
get up

At once she sat up. She was well again.
"She'll need something to eat," said Jesus to her parents.

The Sower

When the crowds came to listen to Jesus, he often told them stories.

"Once," he said, "a man went out to sow seeds. Up and down the field he plodded, flinging handfuls of seeds.

"Some fell on the path. Birds swooped down and ate them.

"Some seeds fell on stony ground. The seeds soon sprouted, but the roots did not go deep.

"When the sun shone bright and hot, the seedlings drooped.

"Some seeds fell among thorn bushes. They soon grew, but the plants could not reach the light. They faded away.

"Other seeds fell on the good brown earth. They grew and produced a good harvest."

flop

peck peck

41

It was a good story, but even Jesus' best friends were puzzled. "What does it mean?" they asked.

"It's about the people who come and listen to me," said Jesus. "Some are like the seeds on the path. They hear my words but don't remember. It's as if the words were snatched away.

Gone

I give up

"Some are like the seeds on stony ground. They hear what I say. They try to obey. Then things get hard and they give up.

42

"Some are like the seeds among thorn bushes. They too try to obey my words. Then everyday worries get in the way.

Have to make money

Let's share

"Others are like the seeds on good brown earth. They hear my words. They obey them. Their lives are a harvest of good deeds."

The Lost Sheep

Jesus told this story.

"There was once a shepherd who had a flock of sheep.

"He counted them every day.

"Then one day when he was counting, there was bad news.

One, two, three

Ninety-nine… Oh!

Take care

"One sheep was missing.

"The shepherd left the ninety-nine sheep in the field.

"He went looking for his lost sheep.

plod

walk

"At last he found it.

baa

There you are

A party!

"The poor thing. The shepherd picked it up and carried it home.

"When it was safely with the flock, he called his friends.

"'Let's celebrate together,' he said.

"'My sheep was lost, and now it's found.'

"Remember this story," said Jesus, "and remember this too:

"People who do wrong things feel lost and alone.

"When they see their mistake, they are friends with God again.

"And all the angels celebrate."

Tra la la

Joy!

The Good Samaritan

A man had a question for Jesus. "What does it mean to love other people?"

Jesus told this story.

"A man was going from Jerusalem to Jericho.

"On the way, robbers attacked him. They beat him up, stole his money, and left him lying in the road.

Help

Ouch

"A priest came by: it was his job to help people worship God in the great Temple in Jerusalem.

"He saw the man in the road. He walked past on the other side.

"Another man came by: it was his job to help the priest.

"He saw the man in the road. He came to look. Then he hurried on.

Oh dear

"A Samaritan came by. Samaritans don't even go to the Temple in Jerusalem.

"He saw the man.

49

heehaw

There there

"He went over to him.

"He bathed his wounds.

"He lifted him onto his donkey.

"He led him to an inn and took care of him. *jingle*

"The next day, the Samaritan had to travel on.

" 'Here is money,' he said to the innkeeper. 'Take care of that man for me. If it costs more, I will pay next time I come.' "

50

Jesus looked at the person who had first asked the question.

"Who showed love in that story?" he asked.

"The one who was kind," came the answer.

Jesus smiled.

You go and do the same

The Merchant and the Pearl

"The most important thing in the world," said Jesus, "is being friends with God.

"What do you do if something is very important?

"Listen to this story.

pink pearls

52

black pearls

"There was once a merchant. He travelled far and wide to find the best pearls.

white pearls

blue pearls

53

"One day, he had the chance to buy an amazing pearl.

"It was big.

"It was pure white.

"It was perfectly round.

"It was very expensive.

"The merchant knew it was the most valuable pearl in the world.

I have to afford it!

"He went off and sold all the pearls he had. Then he came back and bought the pearl that he really loved."

Ooh!

Aah!

Building a Tower

Crowds of people came to listen to Jesus.

"Do you really want to follow me?" he asked. "Then you must love one another.

"You must forgive the wrong things that people do to you.

"You may find it hard."

The people began to wonder if this was a good idea.

Not sure

Hmm

"It's like with any big plan," said Jesus.
"Imagine someone who dreams of building a tower.

*It will be
the tallest!*

"First of all, he must count the cost.

workers

wood

bricks

"If he doesn't, he may run out of money. The tower will be half finished.

"Everyone will see how foolish he was.

"And they will laugh."

Ha ha ha

The Man Who Could Not Pay

That's too kind

One day, Jesus' friend Peter came to him. He had a question.

"If someone keeps treating me badly, how many times should I forgive? Is seven times too much?"

"It's not enough!" replied Jesus. "You must forgive seventy times seven."

Jesus told a story.

"There was once a king. He had lent money to his servants. Now he wanted to know how much they owed.

"There was one who owed him millions.

" 'Please,' begged the servant. 'I can't pay.'

" 'Can't pay?' said the king. 'Then I'll sell you as a slave. I'll sell your family if I need to.'

" 'Please, no – be patient with me,' whimpered the servant.

" 'Oh… all right. I'll let you off,' said the king.

There, there

Sob

"The servant went off. He knew he had been very lucky.

"Then he saw another servant. 'That man owes me money!' he exclaimed. He ran up to him and grabbed him.

" 'Pay me what you owe. Pay me everything. Pay me now.'

"The second servant was dismayed.

" 'Please give me more time,' he pleaded. 'I will pay.'

"The first servant did not show
any pity. He had the second
thrown into jail.

"The king heard what had
happened. He ordered the first
servant to come and see him.

" 'I forgave you an enormous
amount. You should have forgiven
your friend. As you didn't –
off to jail with you!'

"And that," said
Jesus, "is what God
will do if you do
not forgive."

The Rich Fool

One day, a man spoke to Jesus from the crowd.
"I know you are fair and honest. I need you to
tell my brother that he's being unfair. I need you to tell
him to share the money our father left us."

"That's not for me to say," replied Jesus.

He turned to speak to everyone.

Where shall I put the crops?

64

"Don't let yourself become greedy for money. It's not the things you have that matter."

He told a story.

"There was once a man who had a farm. Its fields produced good crops.

" 'There isn't room in my barns for all this,' he said.

"Then he had an idea.

 " 'I'll pull down the old barns and build bigger ones.

 " 'Then I'll be wealthy for ever.

 " 'I'll be able to take life easy.'

Eat! Drink! Be merry!

"He was forgetting: life doesn't go on for ever. Just when he thought he was rich, he died. Someone else got all his money.

"That's what happens. So don't make money the most important thing in life. Make it your aim to live as a friend of God."

For me!
How nice!

The Friend at Midnight

Jesus often spent time saying prayers. His friends asked him to teach them to pray.

"Speak to God as to a loving father," he said.

"Tell God that you want him to be loved and obeyed by everyone.

"Ask God to give you the strength you need.

"Ask God to forgive the wrongs you have done.

"Ask God to keep you from hard times."

Our Father in heaven

Then he told a story.
"Once a man was locking
up his home for the night.
As he stood behind the
door, he heard a knock.

rat tat tat

"He opened the door, and there was a friend.
"'I was passing by on my journey,' cried
the friend. 'I hope I can stay the night.'
"'Of course!' said the man.
'You are welcome.'
"He went to the kitchen.
What food did he have
to offer?

Nothing!

"He slipped out and ran next door. He knocked. He banged. He hammered.

"At last the neighbour stuck his head out of the window. 'Go away! We've all gone to bed,' he grumbled.

RAT TAT TAT

" 'But I need to borrow some food for a friend,' came the reply.

"The neighbour got up and stomped to the door with a basket of food.

"Remember," said Jesus. "Even a grumpy neighbour will do what you want if you ask enough.

"When you ask your Father God, you will be answered."

There

Ten Bridesmaids

"**D**o you want to be friends with God?" Jesus asked his listeners. "Then you must be ready always. No one knows when God will come to meet you.

"Once there were ten bridesmaids.

I brought extra lamp oil in case he's late

You won't need it

"Their task was to welcome the bridegroom.

"He was expected at nightfall. The bridesmaids lit their lamps and waited.

"An hour went past. Two hours.

"The bridesmaids grew tired.

"They began to fall asleep.

"They were woken by a shout.

" 'He's coming! Everyone get ready.'

"The bridesmaids jumped up. The five who had brought extra oil poured it into the lamps to make sure they went on burning brightly.

"The other five had almost no oil left.

" 'Can we have some of yours?' they asked.

We must go and buy more

Can we borrow?

There's none spare

"The five girls who needed more oil hurried away.
While they were gone, the bridegroom arrived.

"The five wise bridesmaids lifted their lamps high.
They cheered as they followed the bridegroom into the feast.

"The five foolish bridesmaids came back too late.
They were not even allowed in.

"So always be ready for God," said Jesus.

The Great Feast

Once Jesus was at a banquet. "This is good," said the man next to him. "But the feast that God gives his friends will be amazing!"

Jesus told a story.

Today's the day!

"There was once a man who arranged a huge feast. He sent a messenger asking his friends if they would come. Then he got everything ready.

"On the day of the feast, the messenger went to remind the guests.

"One by one the guests began to make excuses.

Oh dear!

" 'I've just bought a plot of land. I have to go and see it!'

Sorry

" 'I've bought some oxen. I have to try them out.'

Sorry I forgot

" 'I just got married. I really can't come.'

"When the man found out that the guests weren't coming, he was very upset.

" 'Everything is ready!' he cried. 'There's so much food!

" 'I know what I'll do,' he told his messenger. 'I want you to go into town and find all the poor people – beggars who can't walk, or can't see. Bring them to the feast.'

You're invited

What a treat!

Who, me?

"The guests arrived, but there was still room for more.

" 'Please go out again,' the man asked his messenger. 'Go along the country roads and bring in the people you see.

" 'As for the guests I first chose,' said the man, 'they won't get a taste of this fantastic food.' "

The Runaway Son

I want it now

Some people complained about Jesus. "He doesn't choose his friends well. A lot of his followers are the wrong kind of people." Jesus told a story.

"There was once a man who had two sons. The younger was bored of working on the farm. He wanted to go and have fun in the city.

"'Please let me have my share of the family money,' he said.

"'It will be yours when I die,' said the father.

"The young man didn't want to wait.

Bye

Tra la la

"With a sigh, the father agreed. The young son sold the land that was now his. He went with his money to a city far away. There he enjoyed himself.

"Then the harvests failed. The price of food went up.

"The young man had been extravagant. Now his money had run out.

"He had to go and get a job. The only work he could get was looking after pigs.

"'I'm so miserable,' he wept. 'And hungry. I could eat the pig food.'

"Then he had an idea.

"'I shall go back to my father and say I'm sorry. I shall ask him to hire me as a servant.'

gobble

oink

Hurrah   He's alive

"He set off for home. He still had some way to go when his father saw him... and came running.

"'My son! You're back!' he cried.

"'I'm sorry for what I did,' mumbled the young man. 'Please take me on as a servant.'

"'But I love you!' cried the father. 'Servants... hurry! Get this boy new clothes... and make a feast.

"'We're going to have a party!'"

The Workers in the Vineyard

"One day," said Jesus, "God will welcome his friends into his kingdom. It will be like this."
He told a story.

A good wage

"There was a man who had a vineyard.
The grapes were ripe, so he needed workers to harvest them.
   "He went to the market in the early morning and hired some men.
   " 'I will pay a silver coin each for the day's work,' he said.
   "They accepted.

"At nine o'clock, the man saw how much work was left.

"He went and hired more workers.

Agreed

One silver coin each

"He did the same at noon, and again at three... and then at five.

"When the day was over, everyone lined up to collect their pay.

"Those who had worked the shortest time each got a silver coin. Those who had worked the longest began to hope for more. But they too were paid one silver coin each.

"'We worked for hours!' they complained. 'It was hot during the day. We never stopped. That other lot only worked one hour.'

"'I am being fair,' said the man. 'I am paying what we agreed.'"

Thank you

That's not fair

The Two Builders

The crowds gathered around Jesus.
"Love one another," he told them. "Forgive one another.
"Don't worry about everyday things, but trust in God.
"If you do these things, then you are like the wise builder.
"He chose the very best place for his house.
"It was high on a rock, where the ground was solid.

This is hard work

dig dig

"The rain came.

pitter patter

"The wind blew.

whoo

"The river flooded.

gurgle

"The house stood firm.

89

"If you do not listen to what I say, then you are like the foolish builder.

"He chose the easiest place for his house.

"It was down on the sand, where the ground was soft.

dig dig

This is easy

"The rain came.

pitter patter

"The wind blew.

whoo

"The river flooded.

gurgle

"The house fell down.

FLAT

"What a terrible fall it was!"

God's Kingdom

J esus also told this story about God's kingdom.
"It is like a tiny seed," he said. "You can
hardly see it.

"When it is sown, it grows into a huge tree.
All kinds of birds come and make their home
in its branches."

chirrup

tweet

God's Kingdom

COO